# Under My Feet

Written by Becca Heddle

Illustrated by Roger Stewart

**Collins**

# Under my feet is tarmac.

3

# Under the hard tarmac ...

... is rock and soil.

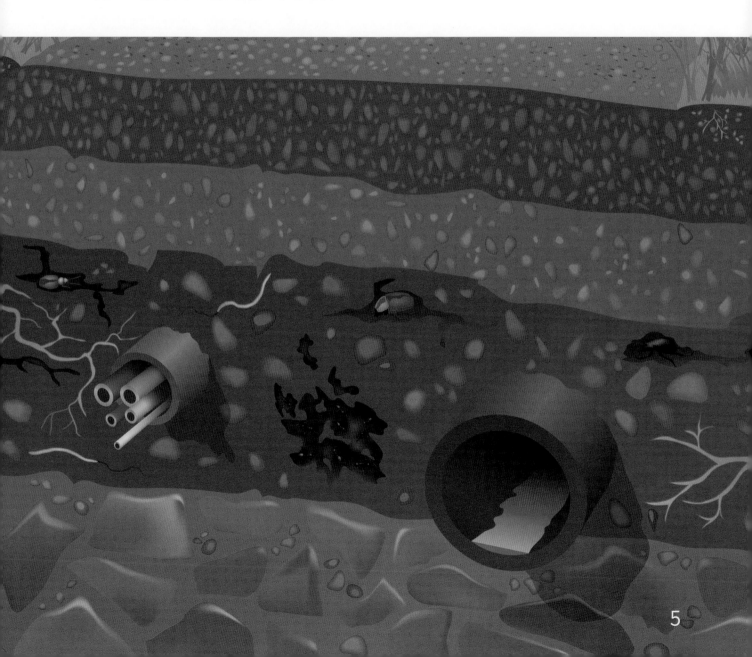

# Under the hill ...

... cars zoom along tunnels.

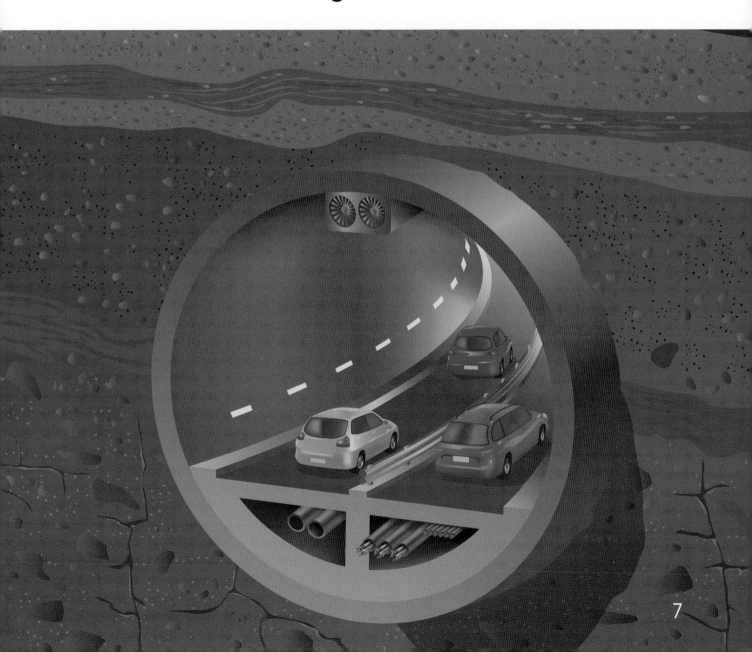

# Under the turf ...

... the soil has roots that soak up rain.

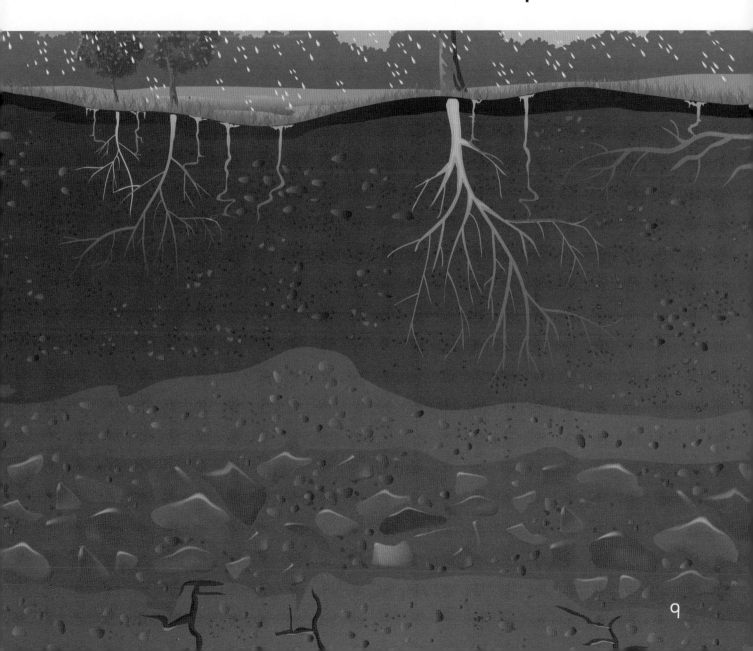

# A fox digs deep down ...

... to dig dens in cool soil.

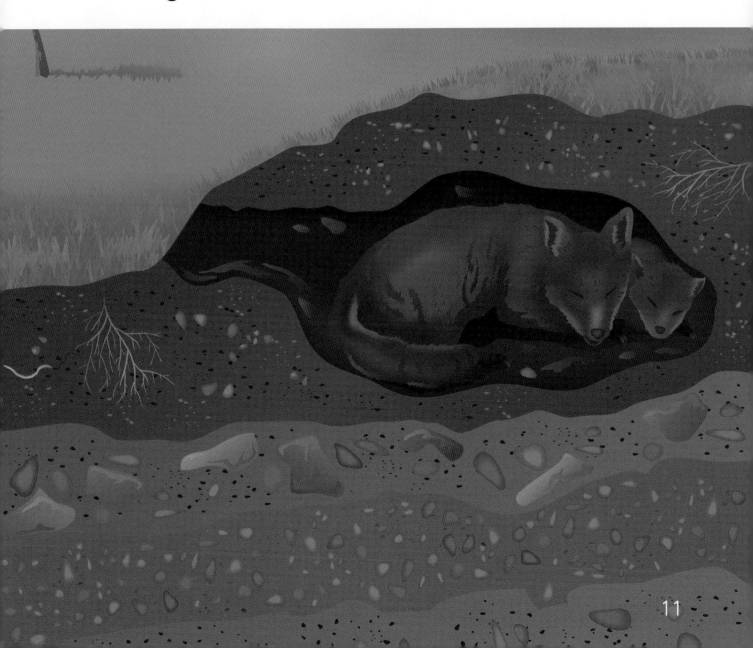

# I cannot see it all ...

... under my feet!

# Under my feet

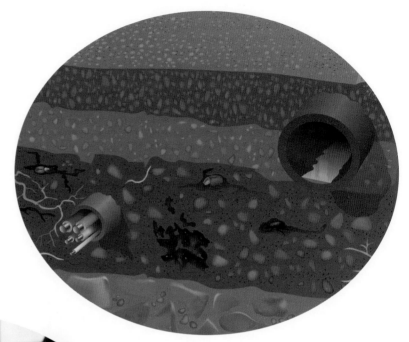

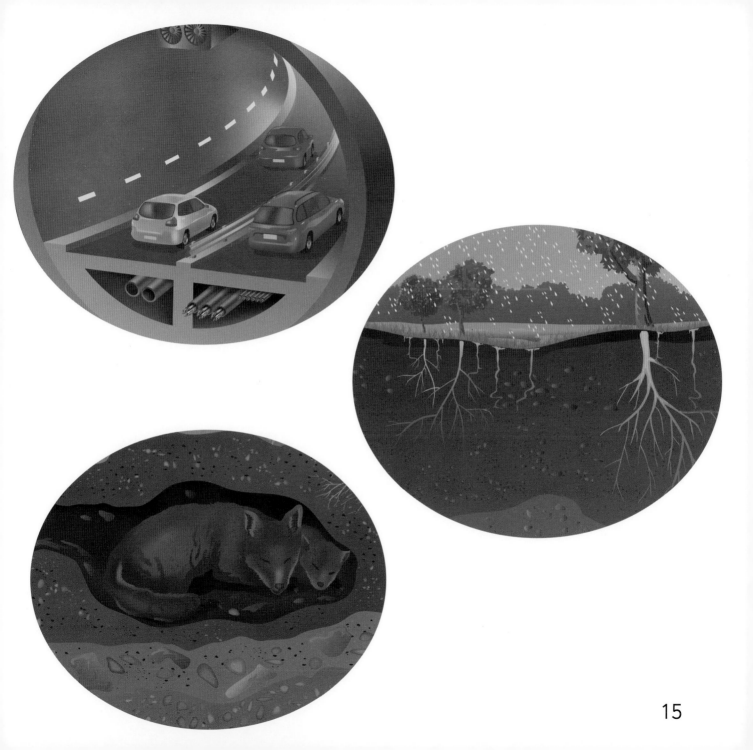

#  Review: After reading

Use your assessment from hearing the children read to choose any GPCs, words or tricky words that need additional practice.

## Read 1: Decoding

- Turn to pages 8 and 9 and focus on the digraphs.
  - Point to **soil** and model sounding it out – **s/oi/l**.
  - Point to the following and ask the children to identify the digraph in each word. Then, ask them to read the words by sounding them out and blending.
    **roots        soak        rain**
- Model reading page 2 fluently. Challenge the children to read it in the same way. Say: Can you blend in your head when you read the words?

## Read 2: Prosody

- Model reading page 6, first without emphasis and then again, emphasising **hill**.
- Discuss the effect. (e.g. *makes it more interesting; clarifies that we're talking about the hill*)
- Ask the children to read page 7. Suggest they emphasise **zoom** so that it sounds like its meaning.

## Read 3: Comprehension

- Ask the children: What is under your feet now? What is deeper down?
- Focus on page 5 and discuss how this is a cutaway to show what's below. Discuss how it shows us things we don't usually see.
- Turn to pages 14 and 15 and encourage the children to talk about the pictures, using words from the book and their own ideas.